Archimedes and His Numbers
Biography Books for Kids 9-12 | Children's Biography Books

Speedy Publishing LLC

40 E. Main St. #1156

Newark, DE 19711

www.speedypublishing.com

Copyright 2017

All Rights reserved. No part of this book may be reproduced or used in any way or form or by any means whether electronic or mechanical, this means that you cannot record or photocopy any material ideas or tips that are provided in this book

Archimedes was one of the greatest scientists and inventors the world has ever known. His curiosity about the world let him discover many things. So, let's take a look at Archimedes and what he discovered.

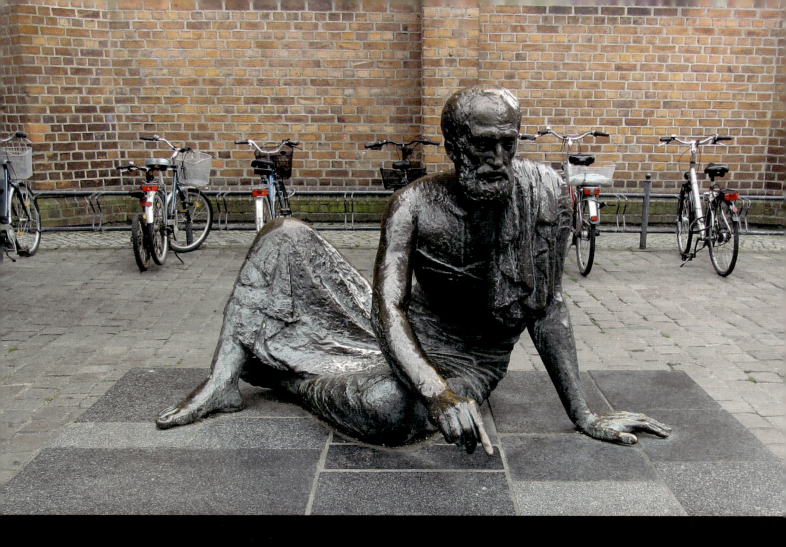

Archimedes was born in the Greek city of Syracuse in Sicily, now part of Italy, about 287 BC. His father was Pheidias, an astronomer.

Archimedes spent most of his life in Syracuse, but he did make at least one trip to Alexandria in Egypt. When he was there, he visited the famous Library and consulted some of its ancient books.

In those days you had to go where the books were, or get copies sent to you; you couldn't just look things up online.

Archimedes exchanged many letters with Eratosthenes, the head of the Library and a great scientist himself. The two inspired each other to look more deeply, and more widely, at the world.

Archimedes explored numbers, physics, engineering, astronomy and weapons design. He followed where his thoughts led him, and sometimes arrived at startling places. Much of what he wrote was lost for hundreds of years.

Mathematicians used to be frustrated with Archimedes because he would often give the answer to a problem without explaining how he got to the answer. Everyone thought his mathematical formulas had been lost.

Then, in 1906, Johan Heiberg found an old Christian prayer book in what is now Istanbul, Turkey.

Heiberg noticed that someone had tried to erase other material from the book before writing prayers in it.

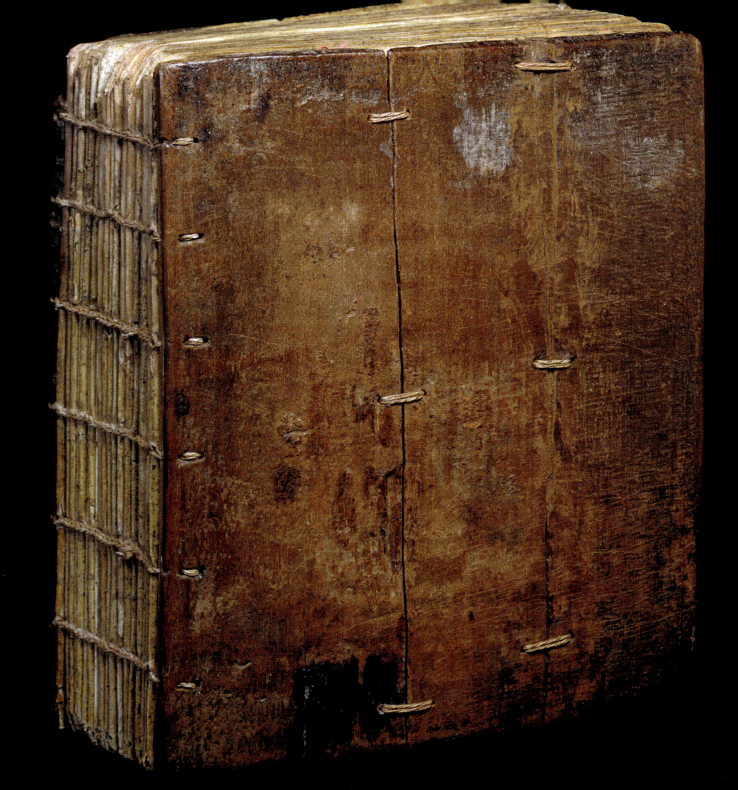

That older material turned out to be a tenth-century copy of Archimedes' The Method, in which he explained how he did mathematics. He had sent the original to his friend Eratosthenes for safe-keeping, but all copies beside this one in the prayer book had been lost or destroyed over the centuries.

Archimedes

Isaac Newton

Archimedes felt his greatest discoveries had to do with numbers and calculations. People rank him as one of the top mathematicians of all time, along with Isaac Newton (1642-1727) and Carl Gauss (1777-1855). Here are some high points:

The Beast Number

Archimedes became annoyed by people saying it would not be possible to count the number of grains of sand in the sea, or the number of drops of water in the ocean, because numbers could not go that high.

The Greek number system was limited, because each number was related to a letter combination, and there were only so many combinations of letters possible. Traditionally, the highest possible number in the Greek system was a "myriad", which we would write as 10,000.

Archimedes got by this problem by developing a whole new number system. He introduced "orders" of numbers, which was like the "powers" system we use today.

Using "powers", we can write "myriad", or 10,000, as 10⁴: this means ten times ten times ten times ten, or "ten to the fourth power".

Archimedes used his "orders" system to show you could count, not just all the grains of sand on the earth, but all the grains of everything in the whole universe. You could write a number big enough to hold all physical matter!

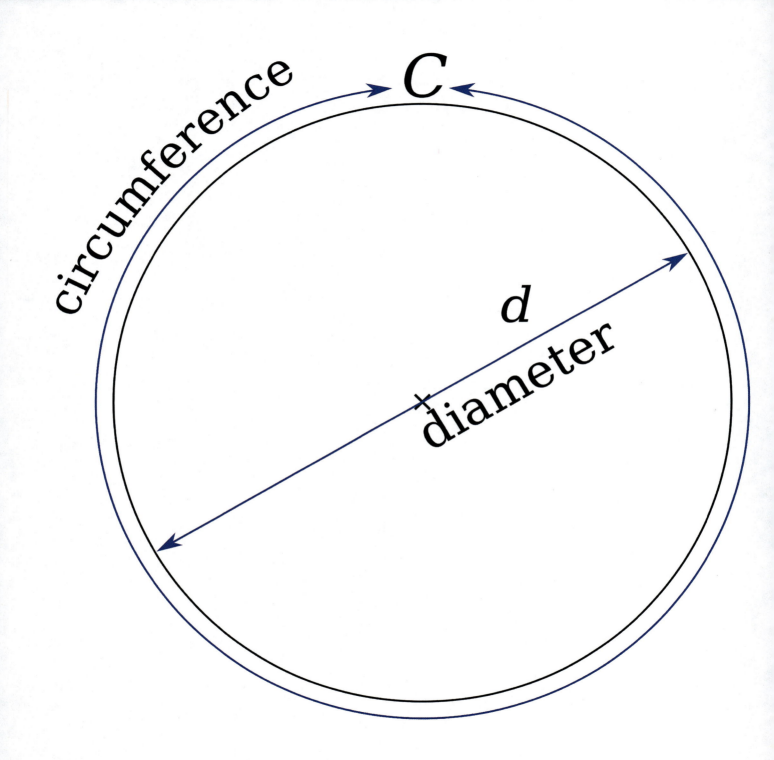

The Value of π (Pi)

If you divide the circumference of a circle by its diameter, you get a value a little bit larger than 3. This value is known as π, the Greek letter pronounced "pi".

If you have either the circumference or the diameter, you can get the other value using π. Archimedes was able to give a very precise value for π: 22/7, or 3.141868115.

This value is so exact that it stayed in use until the invention of computers made even better calculations possible.

Measuring a Sphere

Archimedes considered this his greatest work. He asked that his tomb should have a symbol on it (a sphere inside a cylinder) marking this discovery.

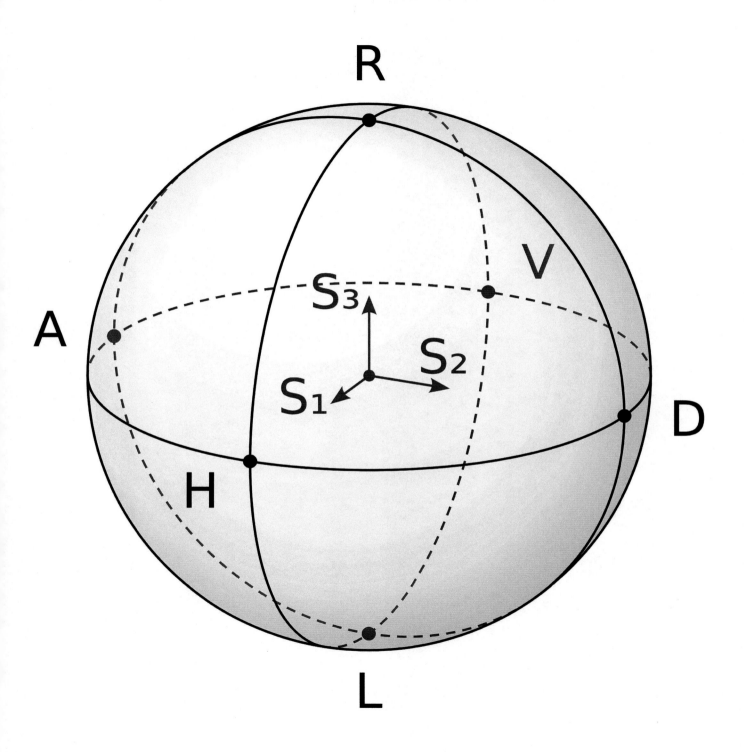

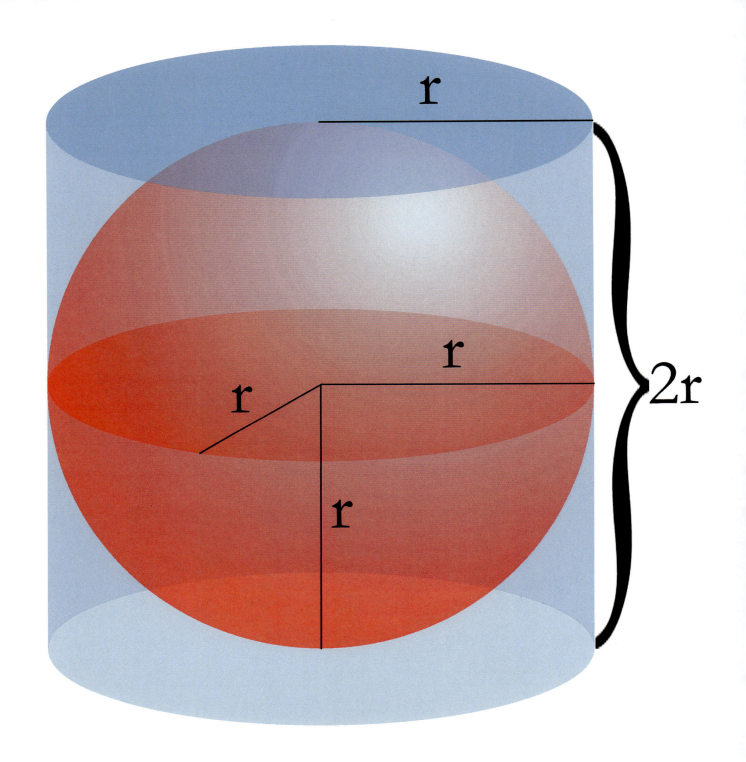

Finding out the volume and surface area of a sphere was hard, because it was hard to know where to start. Archimedes, in a thought experiment, divided a sphere in half so he could work with a hemisphere. This gave him a shape with one flat side, and if he could find its volume and surface area, he could just multiply the answers by two to get the volume and surface area of the whole sphere.

Okay, so now in his imagination Archimedes has a hemisphere inside a cylinder. The width and height of the cylinder are the same as the diameter and radius (the value r, equal to half the diameter) of the sphere. Measuring a cylinder was already known: its volume was $πr^2h$. Since in this example radius (r) and height (h) are the same value, we can simplify the statement to $πr^3$.

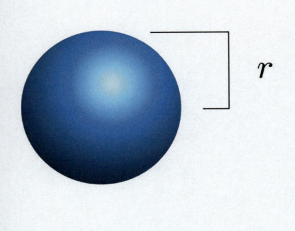
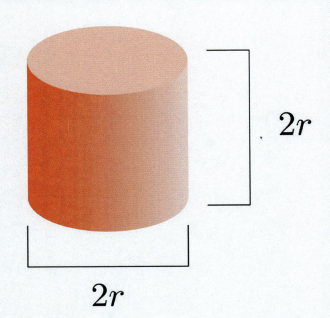

$$\frac{V_{\text{cylinder}}}{V_{\text{sphere}}} = \frac{\pi r^2 \cdot (2r)}{\frac{4}{3}\pi r^3} = \frac{3}{2}$$

$$\frac{A_{\text{cylinder}}}{A_{\text{sphere}}} = \frac{2 \cdot \pi r^2 + 2\pi r \cdot 2r}{4\pi r^2} = \frac{3}{2}$$

So Archimedes knew the volume of the hemisphere would be less than that because the hemisphere was inside the cylinder. But how much less? In his imagination, Archimedes started slicing the cylinder as if he were slicing a round loaf of bread. Each slice had a hole in the middle for the part of that slice that was inside the sphere.

> Archimedes measured the part of each slice that was not inside the sphere, and discovered that it added up to the volume of a cone whose base was the same size as the flat side of the hemisphere, and whose height was the same as the radius of the hemisphere.

Measuring a cone was known: its volume would be $\tfrac{1}{3}\pi r^2 h$, simplified in this experiment to $\tfrac{1}{3}\pi r^3$.

Having gotten to here, Archimedes knew that the volume of the hemisphere would be the volume of the cylinder minus the volume of the cone: πr3 - ⅓πr3, or ⅔πr3. Now that he had the volume of a hemisphere, he showed that the volume of the whole sphere would be two times that, or 4/3 πr3.

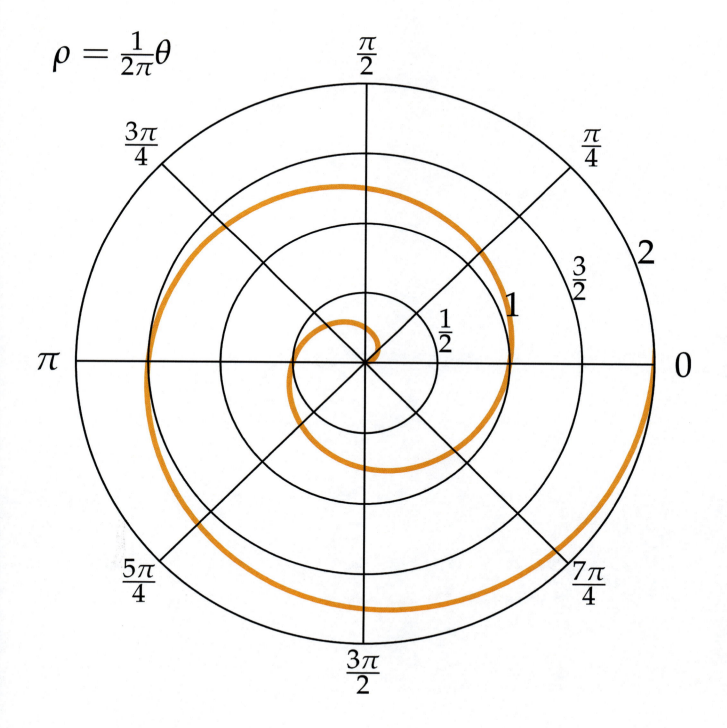

Using the same methods and working from the known formulas for finding the surface area of cylinders and cones, Archimedes showed that the surface area of a sphere would be $4\pi r^2$.

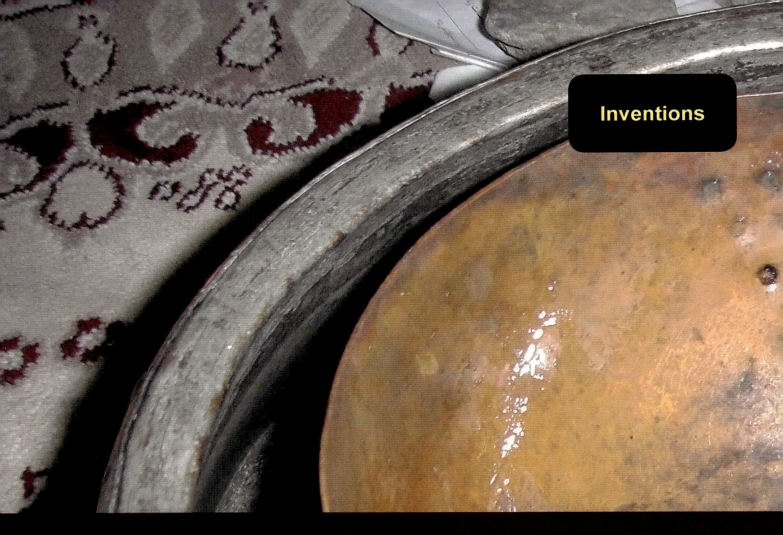

Inventions

A lot of what Archimedes worked on was pure research, without any particular use in mind. However, he was also a practical engineer and the creator of many inventions. Some of what Archimedes invented is still in use today, largely unchanged.

The Water Screw

King Hieron II had Archimedes build him a huge and luxurious boat. The boat could hold 600 people, and even had its own gymnasium and temple.

But the boat was so big that when water leaked in, it was awkward to get it out again. Archimedes invented a screw in a tube, with a crank at the top.

The bottom end of the tube was in the water that gathered in the bottom of the boat. When you turned the crank, gradually the screw lifted the water up to where it was easy to throw it overboard.

Farmers through the centuries have used the same screw design to raise water from irrigation canals so the water can get to their plants.

Inventions

THE CATAPULT

Archimedes designed a catapult that could throw huge rocks toward the enemy army, or over the walls of forts and other defense barriers.

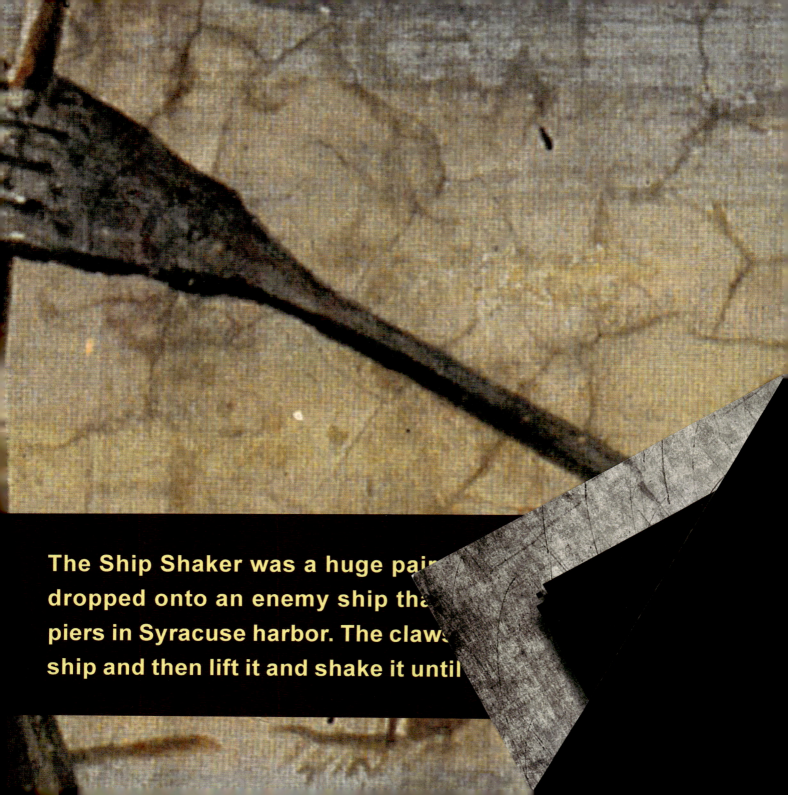

The Ship Shaker was a huge pair
dropped onto an enemy ship tha
piers in Syracuse harbor. The claw
ship and then lift it and shake it until

The Heat Ray

Archimedes designed a huge array of mirrors. In theory, on a bright, still day, if you adjusted all the mirrors so the light each one reflected fell on the same part of a ship's sail, the concentrated sunlight would make the sail burst into flames.

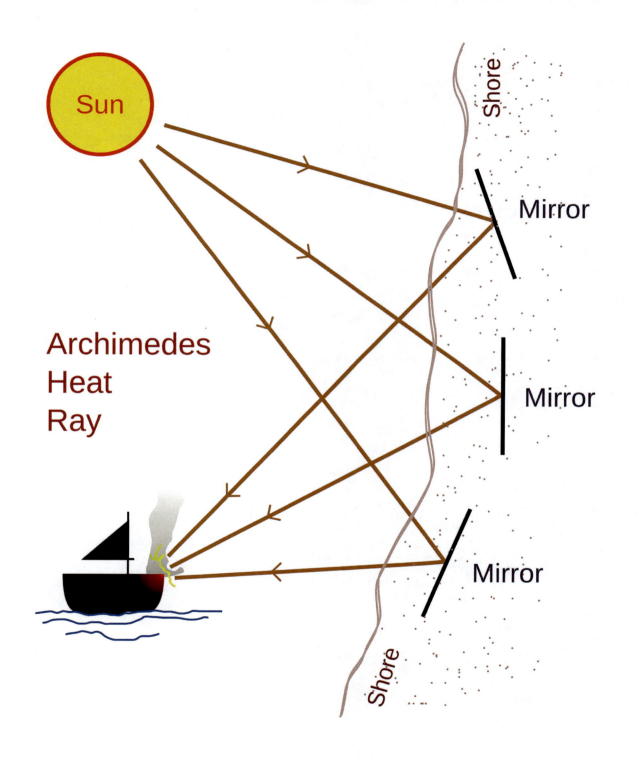

This is one of those great ideas that's really hard to make work in the real world, since the enemy ship is not likely to hold still until you have arranged all the mirrors properly. It was a good plan if weather conditions were perfect, but probably nobody ever tried to really do it.

The Planetarium

Archimedes built two models of the solar system as people knew it in his day, with the sun, earth, moon, and five other planets. The planetarium had gears so when you turned a handle all the planets moved in relation to each other. General Marcellus took the devices back to Rome after he conquered Syracuse.

The Death of Archimedes

When Rome attacked and conquered Syracuse, one of their goals was to capture Archimedes. Rome wanted to use his skills to develop new weapons of war. Archimedes was studying hard when the soldiers arrived at his house, Archimedes was deep in his studies and possibly did not even realize what was going on. He refused to leave his work, and a soldier grew impatient and killed him. Archimedes was 74.

All through history, scholars and scientists have made great discoveries to help all people. Read other Baby Professor books to find out more about other heroes of science!

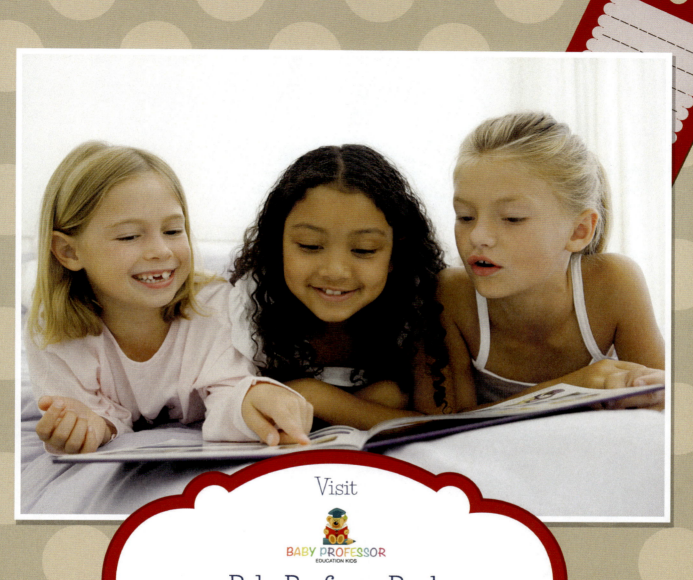